# GLOUCESTER
## IN OLD PHOTOGRAPHS
### FROM THE COUNTY LIBRARY COLLECTION

# GLOUCESTER

## IN OLD PHOTOGRAPHS

### FROM THE COUNTY LIBRARY COLLECTION

COLLECTED BY

## JILL VOYCE

Budding
BOOKS

A Budding Book

First published in 1985 by Alan Sutton Publishing Limited

This edition published in 1998 by Budding Books,
an imprint of Sutton Publishing Limited
Phoenix Mill · Thrupp · Stroud · Gloucestershire GL5 2BU

A catalogue record for this book is available from the British Library

ISBN 1-84015-069-6

Typesetting and origination by
Sutton Publishing Limited.
Printed in Great Britain by
WBC Limited, Bridgend, Mid-Glamorgan.

# CONTENTS

# INTRODUCTION

The pictures in this book have been selected from material in Gloucester Library known as the Gloucestershire Collection, which is freely available for consultation by any member of the public wishing to widen their knowledge of the county and people who were born in Gloucestershire or have a very long connection with it. What a treasure store it is – whether you wish to trace your family history, compile a history of your locality or house, read about the crimes committed and the sentences meted out, find out what was happening on the day you were born, compare the bus, rail or postal services of yesteryear with today or just enjoy the past by looking at old photographs and maps, you will find it fascinating. Collected by library staff since the turn of the century, and enhanced by numerous donations and bequests, the collection now has in excess of 160,000 items and deals with 20,000 enquiries each year from all over the world. Here you will find almost every book written about Gloucestershire, local newspapers (including the only complete set of the *Gloucester Journal* from 1722), guide books and directories, maps, portraits and illustrations, manuscripts dating from the sixteenth century, letters from such notables as Robert Raikes and of course the trivia of everyday life which most people threw away, such as election material, telephone directories, society events and theatre programmes.

Photography has added much to historical records, the oldest reproduced here is that of the Abbot's House pulled down in 1860. At this time the city was much smaller with the boundary running approximately along the Sudbrook in Parkend Road and Southgate Street, to the Quay, river and St Catherine's meadow, crossed London Road near the Welsh Harp Inn and continued along to Barton Gates. Thus the railway and fast growing Barton and Tredworth areas were officially in the county.

Change of course is inevitable, many streets have been widened and altered, many have been renamed (Parkers Row to Brunswick Road, Mitre Street to the Oxbode and Gallows Lane to Denmark Road); many fine town houses have been demolished and open spaces filled, such as James Forbes house for the Co-operative Stores extension, Charlton House for the Public Baths and the Cattle Market for shops and a bus station.

I hope that this small selection of photographs will be an evocation of our county town and give as much pleasure to you as the compilation has given to me.

## SECTION ONE

# Streets

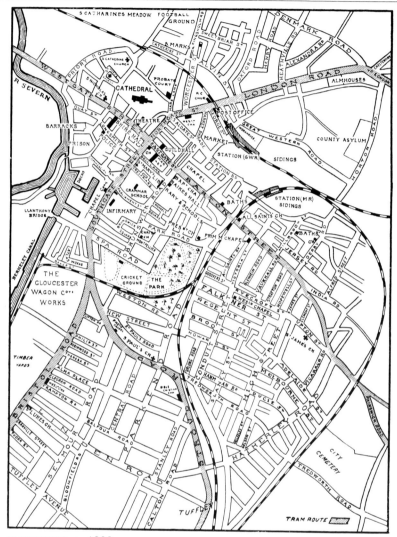

GLOUCESTER, c. 1908.

BARTON STREET, 1913. This building, next door to Staite's Furniture Removers, was taken down on 22nd July 1913. Under the poster for the Eagle Cycle Works is Seyer's Passage.

BARTON STREET. From the Vauxhall Inn to Blenheim Road.

BARTON STREET c. 1923 (now Eastgate Street). This photograph shows, left to right, W.G. Coles' photographic studio and the house of Dr Firmin Cuthbert (set back from the road), sold in 1920 to the Gloucester Co-operative Society for an extension to their premises, seen here before modernisation. The curved archway, covered in vegetation, led to the offices of G.C.P. Pike, Solicitor.

BEARLAND, 1912. An early morning photograph – a lady is scrubbing the steps of the Petty Sessional Court which stood on the corner of Barbican Road. Trigg's, the carpenter and joiner, was pulled down and replaced by the Fire Station, opened 17th July 1913. This is now the Transport Museum. Bearland House on the extreme left was built c. 1735 and has been the High School for Girls, the Telephone Manager's Office and is today occupied by the Preece Payne Partnership.

BERKELEY STREET, c. 1897. Left to right: Arnold, Perrett & Co., wine merchants, the Perfect Thrift Building Society, the City Dairy and Berkeley House. The whole site is now occupied by the Telephone Exchange.

BERKELEY STREET, C. 1923. The building with the wires on the roof was the Telephone Exchange before modernisation and later extension.

COLLEGE COURT, c. 1937. Pitcher is a familiar name to collectors of photographs of Gloucester. Father and son were official photographers to Gloucester Corporation for 50 years. St Michael's Gate was originally the entrance to the lay cemetery of the Abbey. The antiques shop was replaced by British Home Stores, access to their snack-bar could be gained from here.

COLLEGE STREET, C. 1876. College Street, originally only 10 feet 9 inches wide, was widened by the Gloucester Cathedral Approaches Company in the 1890s. The west tower of King Edward's Gate built by Edward I is all that survives. To the left of King Edward's Gate was the servants' registry office. The building still serves today – but as a restaurant.

SOUTHGATE STREET. Viewed from the Cross in the late 1890s immediately after the erection of the first street arc lamp.

DEAN'S WALK, 1909. From the junction with St Catherine Street, widened in 1909.

DEAN'S WAY (north end). This card is post-marked 1919.

EASTGATE STREET, in the late 1890s. The gentleman on the left is standing on the corner of Brunswick Road.

EASTGATE STREET, c. 1925. On the extreme left is Blinkhorn's Shop and on the extreme right the Hippodrome Cinema which was burned down 23rd October 1955.

ELMBRIDGE ROAD, 1939.

KING'S SQUARE, 1933. The scaffolding is for the construction of the Post Office which opened June 1934. In the background the Ebenezer Gospel Hall and the watch and clock business of E.J. Neininger can be seen.

KINGSHOLM ROAD, c. 1906. Taken near the junction with Denmark Road looking towards the toll house on the corner of Sandhurst Road.

LLANTHONY ROAD, 1899. The gateway to Llanthony Priory.

MITRE STREET, C. 1926, which became the Oxbode in the early 1930s.

NEWTON ROAD (NOW AVENUE), c. 1900. The timbered building was the Primitive Methodist Mission Hall.

NORTHGATE STREET, c. 1898. From the Cross.

NORTHGATE STREET, C. 1923. At the junction of Worcester Street looking towards St Peter's Church. The block of the Coffee House Branch No. 4 to the Theatre De Luxe has been replaced with modern shops.

NORTHGATE STREET, C. 1935.

THE OXBODE, c. 1935. Looking towards Northgate where the Fifty Shilling Tailors and the mock Tudor premises of Boots the Chemists, built immediately before the First World War, can be seen. The Bon Marché, Debenhams as it now is, was built in the early 1930s.

PARK ROAD, c. 1910.

PODSMEAD ROAD, 1906. Photographed 18th January looking south from Tuffley Avenue. The road, not yet surfaced, is full of ruts and puddles.

THE QUAY, taken before the First World War when still a working quay. The buildings facing the river have been replaced by the quayside wing of the Shire Hall and a stone wall now blocks the open aspect across Castle Meads.

ST ALDATE SQUARE. No. 9 Gloucester's first Post Office run by Frederick Woodcock was here from 1822 until c. 1847. The main Post Office was at the Tolsey 1844–92 when it transferred to the Corn Exchange. The earliest town postmen wore red coats and tall hats with cockades which became known as 'rhubarb forcers'.

ST ALDATE STREET, 1928. At the junction of King Street and Market Parade immediately before the redevelopment of what we now call King's Square. Buildings from left to right: Rowland Adams fruiterers, Blandford catering requisites, a shop offering 2 valve wireless sets with 2 loudspeakers installed for £7, a hairdressing and shaving saloon, St. Aldate's Restaurant with accommodation for commercials and cyclists, and, directly behind the ornate lamp standard, Pearce Pope the auctioneer.

ST CATHERINE'S STREET, C. 1897. The building on the extreme left was the First Sunday School for Boys founded by Robert Raikes, whose father founded the *Gloucester Journal* in 1722. Only the row of 8 houses on the centre right are standing today. The pub on the left, whose sign reads Stroud Brewery and Co Entire, was the Queen's Head.

ST JOHN'S LANE, 1920. From Westgate Street looking towards St John's Church, showing the bridge which formerly linked two parts of the *Citizen* and *Journal* offices.

ST CATHERINE'S KNAPP, 1905. The building on the right, where the fishmonger Mr Parsons traded for many years, still stands today and was used as a location in the T.V. serial *Pennies from Heaven*. The timber-framed building on the left carried a plaque stating that it was the first Girls Sunday School founded by Robert Raikes.

SOUTHGATE STREET, c. 1888. Taken from Commercial Road looking towards the Cross.

SOUTHGATE STREET, 1905. The photographer was standing near the Bell Hotel. This was taken prior to the widening of Longsmith Street.

SOUTHGATE STREET, late 1900. The Cross to Baker's, the jeweller. Fredk. Wright the County Cigar Store was the sole agent for Muratti's celebrated 'Ariston' cigarettes as supplied to the Prince of Wales. He also acted as a parcel receiving office for the Midland Railway. A sign to the right of the beautiful gas light advertises the National Telephone Company's call room. The company shortly afterwards marked public call offices by the sign of a blue bell. The now familiar national figures of Baker's clock were not installed until 1904. The barrel of the clock here has written on it 'time ball falls daily at 12 o'clock' and the barometer under is 'set at 9 a.m. daily'.

TUFFLEY CRESCENT, 1906. Photographed 18th January looking towards Tuffley Avenue, prior to the re-laying of the sewer.

WESTGATE STREET, 1897.

WESTGATE STREET, c. 1907. Fletcher's cutlers and gunsmith shop was next door to where MacDonald's is today. At a banquet given in Gloucester for Sir Samuel Baker who had discovered the source of the White Nile, the explorer stated that, apart from his wife and a negro boy, his only companion was his faithful rifle and it was 'the truest little weapon I ever had, and was made by Thomas Fletcher of Gloucester'.

WORCESTER STREET, c. 1905. On the extreme left two men are standing outside George Symonds' cab, omnibus and funeral carriage establishment. The bridge is the 'new one' completed 27th April 1902.

LONGSMITH STREET, 1927. There is very little evidence of mechanisation in this widening and resurfacing operation. The workers of Messrs Greaves, Bull and Lakin are preparing the surface for 'Vitocrete' to be laid.

# SECTION TWO

# Buildings

NO. 4 BARTON STREET. The residence of Dr James Forbes, the first Unitarian Minister in Gloucester 1699–1712. It was demolished in 1921 to make way for an extension to the Co-operative Society.

CITY TEA WAREHOUSE, SOUTHGATE STREET, C. 1910. Was also known as the 'Old Blue Shop', so named either from the manufacture of cake-blue on the premises and the front having been painted blue to advertise it, or the owner was such an ardent Tory that he had it painted blue. Today it is a restaurant and shoe shop.

CONSTITUTION HOUSE. Built 1759 on the corner of Queen Street. When William Montague lived here it is asserted that Gladstone and Disraeli dined here (Gladstone's father lived in Sherborne House). The Conservative Club was opened here 7th August, 1883.

THE CROSS, 1892. The Old Tolsey, or town hall, which stood on the corner of Westgate and Southgate streets derived its name from the collection of tolls for fairs and markets by the City Council. Built in 1751 it was pulled down in 1892 after the building of the Guildhall. At this time the Post Office was housed in the basement and for a short time in 1892 it served as temporary offices for the editorial staff of the *Citizen* whilst the newspaper offices were being built.

DUKE OF NORFOLK'S LODGING, WESTGATE STREET, c. 1904. Occupied by the Duke during his second term as Mayor in 1798, it has been variously a boarding school, cabinet maker's, baker's, butcher's and greengrocer's. Becoming a lodging house in 1902 it was allowed to decay beyond repair and was demolished in October 1971 to be replaced with 'The Dukeries'.

EASTGATE STREET, 1888. Old house taken down March 1888 to make way for National Provincial Bank. At one time it was thought to have been the town residence of Crawley-Boeveys and at another time occupied by Mrs Delany, a friend of Queen Charlotte, wife of George III.

FIRE STATION, BEARLAND. Opened on Tuesday, 17th September 1913 it is now the Transport Museum.

FOLK MUSEUM, WESTGATE STREET. Mr Johnston-Vaughan erected the tablet on the front of the building and later conveyed the house to the Corporation. Traditionally identified as Bishop Hooper's last lodging place, research by the Civic Trust suggests he may have stayed at the Crown Inn next door.

HARE LANE, C. 1930. The plaque reads 'The Old Raven Tavern in which the Hoare family were born. They sailed to America in the Mayflower. They all rose to distinction. From this family the distinguished HOARE member of the legislature of AMERICA descended.' Research has shown that, although in the ownership of the family, it was not the birthplace of the American branch, and that the Raven Tavern was in Southgate Street.

BISHOP JOHN HOOPER (second Bishop of Gloucester 1551–55). The Protestant Bishop was burned at the stake on St Mary's Knapp, 9th February 1555. This new memorial was formally inaugurated on 9th February 1863.

GLOUCESTER INFIRMARY, c. 1898. The Infirmary was designated the Gloucester Royal Hospital when Edward VII visited the City in 1909. On its 250th anniversary, Queen Elizabeth II visited the hospital.

THE KING'S BOARD OR BUTTER MARKET, which formerly stood in Westgate Street and now stands in Hillfield Gardens.

THE OLD CUSTOM HOUSE ON THE QUAY.

'ROBERT RAIKES HOUSE', SOUTHGATE STREET, c. 1890, and on the extreme left the Ram Hotel, now the New County Hotel.

PRICE MEMORIAL HALL, 1900, which houses the Museum. On the left is Jennings, the printers, and on the right the Weights and Measures Office.

ROUND HOUSE ON THE QUAY. Erected c. 1675 as a glass house it was formerly a much taller conical-shaped building. It was demolished in August 1933 to given better access to the premises of the West Midland Farmers' Association from the quay. The name was perpetuated in the Round House Cafe, which stood close by, on the corner of Westgate Street and the Quay.

ST BARTHOLOMEW'S HOSPITAL, 1929. Founded in the reign of Henry III, this building erected in 1786 provided accommodation for 40 elderly residents. The central section was a chapel. It has now been converted into small craft shops.

SCRIVENS' CONDUIT, which formerly stood opposite the Bell Hotel and now stands in Hillfield Gardens.

SUFFOLK HOUSE, GREYFRIARS, c. 1865, whose lawns became the Bowling Green, had been a school, the Liberal Club, the Junior Library and Register Office before being demolished to make way for the present market. The building to the left was Friars' Orchard (the Crypt School).

# Church and Chapel

BISHOP'S PALACE. This photograph, taken from the Cathedral gardens, shows the building demolished prior to 1862 to make way for the Bishop's Palace (erected by Ewan Christian) which in 1955 became part of the King's School.

There appears to have been some reconstruction of the Infirmary Arches on the extreme left. Through the arches the 'new' building can be seen.

CATHEDRAL – SOUTH PORCH, 1860, prior to restoration when the sundial and niches were filled with figures of St Peter, St Paul and the four Evangelists carved by J.F. Redfern. In the niches either side of the doorway figures of King Osric and Abbot Serlo, the founders of the Abbey Church, were placed.

BRUNSWICK BAPTIST CHURCH AND SCHOOL. The church, standing on the site of a previous chapel and schoolroom, opened in 1873. The schools adjoining, erected as a memorial to Robert Raikes, opened in 1884.

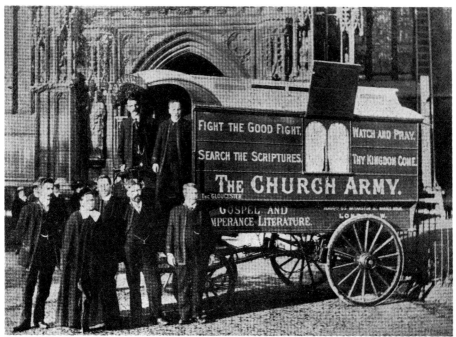

CHURCH ARMY OFFICIALS at the dedication of the Church Army Mission Van for the Gloucester Diocese, 31st October 1905.

NORTHGATE WESLEYAN CHAPEL. The original entrance to the Wesleyan Chapel in Northgate Street, facing Worcester Street ...

... and the Italianate styled building which replaced it in 1878. This church was demolished in the 1970s to make way for Tesco's Stores.

PARK STREET MISSION ROOM. Two cottages purchased in 1678 for a Meeting House for the Society of Friends. It was their only place of worship in Gloucester until the opening of the present Meeting House in Greyfriars in 1834. George Fox and William Penn are said to have preached in this house.

RYECROFT WESLEYAN CHAPEL, CONDUIT STREET. Erected in 1870, and used latterly as an annexe to the College of Art.

ST ALDATE'S CHURCH, ST ALDATE'S STREET, c. 1900. Re-erected 1730.

ST CATHARINE'S CHURCH, PRIORY ROAD. Erected in the Early French Gothic style in 1867–9 on the site of an earlier church which belonged to the Priory of St Oswald, demolished at the time of the Great Rebellion in 1645.

ST JOHN'S CHURCH, NORTHGATE STREET. With its 'leaning spire', truncated in 1910 by W. Larkins, Steeplejack of Bow, which now rests in St Lucy's Gardens. The tower and spire date from the fourteenth century whilst the body of the church was rebuilt in 1732. The railings and cabbies' shelter have long since disappeared.

ST MARY'S HALL SUNDAY SCHOOL. Demolished in 1958. This was used as a playhouse prior to its purchase in 1788 by the Countess of Huntingdon and then for many years was used for the dissemination of the doctrines of George Whitefield.

ST MARY DE CRYPT CHURCH, SOUTHGATE STREET. Photographed prior to 1910 when the pinnacles on the tower were removed. In this church Whitefield was baptised and preached his first sermon in 1736. It also contains the tombs of Robert Raikes, of Sunday School fame, and Jemmy Wood, the eccentric millionaire banker.

ST MICHAEL'S CHURCH. The chancel of this ancient church taken down in 1956. Only the tower, built c. 1465, remains today as the Tourist Information Centre.

ST NICHOLAS'S CHURCH, C. 1902.

ST PETER'S R C CHURCH, NORTHGATE STREET c. 1866. This was rebuilt 1860–8 during the pastorate of Canon Calderbank who received £1,000 for this purpose from Miss Frances Canning of Hartpury. The elegant 156ft high tower and spire was later enhanced by a clock, the gift of the non-Catholic Mayor of Gloucester, W. Viner-Ellis.

Make a new beginning
and mingle again
the kindred
of the nations in
the alchemy of love.

UNITARIAN CHAPEL, BARTON STREET, which stood opposite the Co-op, was built in 1699 by the Rev. James Forbes, a former preacher at the Cathedral who was ejected under the Act of Uniformity.

ST LUCY'S HOME OF CHARITY, HARE LANE, was for a Sisterhood of the Church of England whose work was to tend the sick, comfort the dying and help those in need. The girls' orphanage and industrial home run by this charity provided both a home and training which would gain them work in service. Before demolition, the building was used as a store by the Bon Marché (now Debenhams).

The lawns at the rear are now St Lucy's Gardens at the junction of Hare Lane and Pitt Street.

The kitchen.

The wash house.

SOUTHGATE CONGREGATIONAL CHURCH CHOIR, 1913. Gathered to celebrate Mr Franklin Higgs' jubilee as organist.

## SECTION FOUR

# Disasters

ARMSTRONG EXECUTION. One of the last executions at Gloucester Gaol took place on Derby Day, 31st May 1922, when Herbert Rowse Armstrong of Hay-on-Wye was hanged at 8 o'clock for the murder of his wife by arsenical poisoning. He had been condemned to death at Hereford Assizes and brought to Gloucester as Hereford Prison had been closed down.

SID BROWN'S FUNERAL, 8th April 1926. There were over 1,000 mourners at the funeral of the Gloucester City and County rugby player who died following an operation after having been injured in a game against Aberavon at Kingsholm. The funeral cortège had started from his father's home on Bloomfield Road for the service in All Saints' Church.

DOCKERS' STRIKE, 1926. Under emergency powers taken during the General Strike, thirteen dock workers were each sentenced to fourteen days' hard labour for preventing the working of the canal bridge at Hempsted. The top picture shows the crowds outside the police court in Bearland, at that time next to the old fire station. The building on the extreme left was replaced firstly by the former County Library H.Q. and today by the Telephone Exchange. The bottom picture shows the prisoners being escorted by the police to Gloucester Prison.

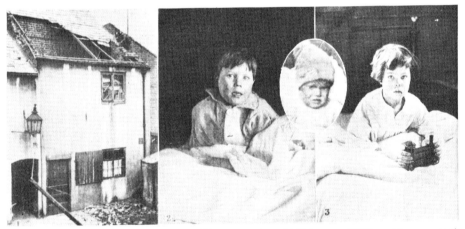

ACCIDENT. During a gale which swept Gloucester in mid-February 1928 a chimney stack crashed through the roof of No. 1 Sweetbriar Street, killing one and injuring two small children of Mr and Mrs Sidney George Robinson.

WAGON WORKS STRIKE. 1500 men went on strike for a day on 4th October 1911. They were required by management to keep time-boards and book each operation to enable contract costings to be more accurately made; but the men argued that if they were 'book-keeping' they were not on the production line and therefore not earning. This dispute was settled by introducing a time-keeper. Taken outside the works in Bristol Road, the photograph also shows the 20ft high Nelson-Foster Memorial Fountain erected in 1903 at a cost of £277. Thomas Nelson-Foster, a member of the family who owned Foster Oil and Cake Mills, died on 2nd October 1902 whilst on a business trip to South America. The memorial, looking a little dilapidated, now stands in Sydenham Gardens, Stroud Road.

KING EDWARD'S FUNERAL. King Edward VII's funeral day, 20th May 1910. The Recorder, Mayor, Sheriff and Corporation returning to the Guildhall after a service in the Cathedral. The King died on 6th May 1910.

PALMERS ½d. MEALS. For the ninth season E.T.C. Palmer of Hopewell Street on 29th November 1912 commenced selling ½d. meals for out-of-work and poor Gloucestrians. With Mr Stephens (in the bowler) can be seen left to right J. Hall, P. Prosser, J. Griffiths, Mrs Trenfield and Miss Spence.

CONVICTS' ESCAPE. Escapes from prison are few but on the night of 25th October 1906 five convicts escaped from Gloucester Prison and ran to the river where they commandeered the boat of Henry Bubb, forcing him to row them to Castle Meadow. They were at large for several weeks before being apprehended, hiding in a haystack, by P.C.s Wiltshire and Hazel and Inspector Seabright of the Lydney Police.

FLOOD FUNERAL. Flooding was a regular occurrence of winter and spring. When Mr Edwin Watts, landlord of the Jolly Waterman Inn, Sandhurst, died in December 1907 the undertaker (Harris of Worcester Street) had to convey the body and members of his family across flooded meadows to dry land near Kingsholm Close, and by hearse to the Cemetery. By an extraordinary coincidence the funeral of Mrs Watts, who had died 4 years earlier, took place in similar circumstances.

FLOODS, c. 1930. The photograph shows Carter's Yard (off Swan Lane) at the rear of the Old Dial Inn. The people are (right to left) Mrs Florence Knight, daughter Joan (aged 7–8), another daughter, Mrs Apperley, daughter René. The property was owned by Mr Speck.

FLOODS: LOWER QUAY STREET, C. 1930. As she stands outside Mr Spiers' house next to the coal yard, Fanny Creese can be seen raising her jug or pot to the photographer, whilst a swan forages close by, quite unconcerned.

WALKER'S FIRE. Walker's Drapery Store in Eastgate Street was completely gutted, and Parsons ironmongers and Smith, Rogers pork butchers seriously damaged when fire broke out on Sunday, 1st October 1911. The fire spread quickly because the divisions between the shops were, in places, only boarded up windows. To add to the problem the fire brigades of Gloucester, Cheltenham and Stroud had difficulty getting enough water – it was 20 minutes before the town waterman had cycled in from Barnwood to turn on the water. Parsons' shop was on the corner of Queen Street and was eventually replaced by C&A.

MATTHEW'S FIRE. On the evening of 23rd July 1912 one of the largest fires ever seen in Gloucester broke out at J.A. Matthew & Co., cabinet makers, in High Orchard and Llanthony Road. The 400 ft long factory costing £30,000 was destroyed, 9 houses in High Orchard gutted and 6 houses in Exhibition Street severely damaged. The sparks set alight Walter Colwell's livery stables 'Spa Mews' in St Luke Street and the valuables from St Luke's

Church were removed as the church was so near to the fire. The blaze could be seen from as far away as Cranham. The new City Fire Engine was not available because of gearbox trouble, so it was left to the Stroud and Cheltenham Brigades to bring the blaze under control. Approximately 200 men were put out of work by the fire and most of them also lost the tools by which they earned their living. Sadly, George Massey of 10 High Orchard Street was away at the time leaving his house locked – he lost everything – home, job and tools.

ACCIDENTS appear to have been a frequent occurence in Southgate Street, especially near the junction with Commercial Road, as these four photographs taken in 1926 show.

GENERAL STRIKE, May 1926. Strikers in Commercial Road outside the Employment Exchange. In the centre the Prison Governor's office can be seen.

# The Royal Show

King Edward VII's visit to Gloucester on Wednesday 23rd June 1909 was surely one of the most colourful royal visits made to the city. The occasion was the meeting of the Royal Agricultural Society of England whose show was held on Alney Island (the Castle Mead, Oxleaze and Port Ham section) 22nd to 26th June. Apart from the Jubilee exhibition at Windsor, it was the largest of the 70 shows the Society had arranged since 1838.

Access to the show ground was via a bridge built especially for the occasion from the Quay to Castle Mead. The picture shows the bridge being built on 19th April. Three iron girders have been dropped by T.B. Cooper and Co. (Bristol) on to timber abutments from lighters, as the tide receded in the river.

Gloucester was garlanded with grand decorations and triumphal arches set up by Conway, Jones & Co. of Northgate Street, James Pain & Co. of London and the traders of Gloucester. What anxious moments there must have been on the 22nd when heavy rain fell. Thankfully it did not spoil the decorations as these early morning scenes taken in Eastgate and Westgate Streets show.

The King arrived on the Royal train at the Great Western station at 12.10 p.m.

After inspecting the guard of honour and the veterans (men who were serving in the navy or army before 1862) the King proceeded via Station Road ...

... and Clarence Street to the Guildhall where he received the loyal address by the Mayor, Councillor James Bruton.

From Guildhall the route taken was to Brunswick Square (via Southgate Street and the Spa) where the King was cheered by 7,000 schoolchildren ...

... along Brunswick Road ...

... via Eastgate and Westgate Streets to the Royal Pavilion at the show ground for lunch ... which consisted of melon gonzalez, œufs en cocette à la soubise, filets de sole à l'Anglaise, noisette de mouton à l'epicurien, poulardes de Surrey, salade, jambon d'York froid, délice de fraises glacé, friandises, pêches and coffee. This was accompanied by 5 wines, including an 1824 champagne, and liqueurs.

S MAJESTY the KING
LOS'TER. JUNE 23rd.09
LEAVING the STATION

ETCHES.
WESTON-S-MA

After touring the showground, the King visited the Cathedral before departing by train to Paddington at 4.26 p.m., arriving in London at 6.40 p.m.

# SECTION SIX

# Employment

BOTHERWAY'S BAKERY, KING STREET, 1925.

CARLTON, 29 BARTON STREET. Started in 1894 by Arthur Carlton, it is one of the oldest boot and shoe repairers in Gloucester. They even had shoes sent from Ireland, as some Domestic Science students continued to use the service after leaving College.

CRYPT HOUSE PRESS LTD, BELL LANE, 1925. The Headquarters of the firm which printed Gloucester Library's *Gloucestershire Collection Catalogue*, the weekly newspaper *The Gloucestershire Chronicle* and many hundreds of guides.

THE CO-OPERATIVE SOCIETY. The early story of the Co-operative Society in Gloucester is one of prosperity and rapid expansion. Established by 54 working railwaymen on 10th July 1860, by 1900 it had a membership of 8,600, 18 shops and an 8½ acre site in India Road. This is their first shop, opened in Prince Street, 10th August 1860.

The building on the corner of Eastgate Street was opened 20th September 1877.

No. 4 Branch, Stroud Road, opened 1876.

No. 10 Branch, High Street, Tredworth, opened 1888.

GLOUCESTER SHIRT COMPANY, MAGDALA ROAD, established 1882. 150 girls in the machine room on the first floor were photographed in 1910 making the company's latest style — a Coronation, hem-stitched, fancy-front shirt in white or coloured fabrics.

HAINE AND CORRY, COAL AND BUILDERS' MERCHANTS, THE DOCKS, c.1910.

JENNINGS GUILDING & CO., c. 1927 with a display of the Gloster Standard Dustbin outside their Northgate Street shop (now Bristol & West Building Society).

LEA & CO., NORTHGATE STREET/ST ALDATE STREET, c. 1920. Cabinet and furniture manufacturers occupying almost the whole length of St Aldate Street with four tiers of showrooms. The site was previously occupied by 'The Old Curiosity Shop'.

BADHAM & CO., IRONMONGERS, SOUTHGATE STREET. Having traded for 130 years, this shop, standing next to the Liverpool & London & Globe Insurance Co., near the Bell Hotel, closed during the Bell redevelopment in the 1960s.

T.G. HALL'S CYCLE SHOP, BARTON STREET. This is now Brunel's who remind us of the cycle shop by displaying photographs of the City Cycling Club in which the Hall family play a prominent part.

H.E. JONES, PHOTOGRAPHER, NORTHGATE STREET. Standing where Sainsbury's and the Halifax Building Society now stand.

MORELAND'S MATCH FACTORY, BRISTOL ROAD, c. 1925.

EASTGATE MARKET, opened 29th April 1856, was dismantled in the 1960s and re-erected a little lower down. This shows it in its original position between Eastgate Vaults on the left and Bank House on the right. Many will remember Fitch's Coffee Bar, Embling's sweet, Pole's cheese and butter and Rigby's fish stalls.

THE WHOLESALE MARKET, which was close by the railway station, was opened in November 1928.

SHEEP AND CATTLE MARKET, established 1855 on the site of today's Bus Station. Beautiful plane trees shaded the animals awaiting sale by Bruton Knowles or Pearce Pope, the auctioneers.

Would-be purchasers at Bruton Knowles' sheep sale in 1886.

POST OFFICE SORTING OFFICE, GEORGE STREET, c. 1910.

ROMAN'S TIMBER YARD, THE DOCKS, C. 1901. This area had been a timber yard since 1828. For some years it was used by Price Walker and Co., before it was taken over by Roman's.

WELLINGTON HALL MODEL DAIRY, LONGSMITH STREET, 1928.

# High Days and Holidays

BOOTS ORCHESTRA. This quartet, photographed on 23rd July 1932, entertained diners in the restaurant of Boots the Chemists, who had a shop (with a mock Tudor façade) in Northgate Street, opposite the Oxbode.

THREE CHOIRS FESTIVAL. The orchestra and chorus are seen here with their conductor, Sir Herbert Brewer.

EMPIRE DAY CELEBRATIONS IN THE PARK, Thursday, 23rd June 1910. Empire Day was a day set aside throughout the British Empire for the celebration of Queen Victoria's birthday (24th May). It was re-named Commonwealth Day in 1958 and from 1966 has been celebrated on the Queen's official birthday.

MISSIONARY DEMONSTRATION, 4th June 1908. The great Missionary Demonstration procession is seen here by the Guildhall on their way to the Cathedral. The Archdeacons of Gloucester and Cirencester, attended by their registrars, in front; eleven colonial bishops, with local clergymen acting as chaplains, behind; and the Archbishop of Brisbane and the Bishop of Gloucester, with chaplains and registrar, bringing up the rear.

WATER SUPPLY. The Mayor and Corporation at the Cross on 1st July 1896 at the inaugural ceremony of the new water supply scheme from Newent. This had involved sinking a well 11 feet in diameter and 168 feet deep and constructing a pumping station at Oxenhall, laying a gravity main to Gloucester and constructing a reservoir at Madam's Wood.

OVILLERS-LA-BOISSELLE. Some of the heaviest trench warfare experienced by the 1/5th Glosters on the Western Front was near the village of Ovillers-la-Boisselle, lying 3 miles from Albert on the main road to Bapaume. After the war it became Gloucester's adopted village and on 23rd October 1922 the Mayor of Gloucester formally handed over to the commune a gift of two windmill pumps and reservoirs as the foundation of its new water supply. In October 1925, during a visit by representatives of Ovillers, a wreath was laid on the Gloucester War Memorial in the Park.

SECOND MOP FAIR, 7th October 1907, on the Oxleaze.

LAYING THE FOUNDATION STONE OF ST CATHERINE'S, WOTTON, Tuesday, 28th May 1912, with full Masonic ceremonial. Standing to the right of the stone are the Provincial Grand Master of Gloucestershire the Rt Hon. Viscount St Aldwyn and on his right his deputy, R.V. Vassar-Smith, who was also chairman of the Gloucester Church Extension Society.

THE LIBRARY, BRUNSWICK ROAD. Laying the foundation stone on 16th September 1895 by the Mayor, Alderman Albert Estcourt. On the left of the macebearer (whose mace can be seen outlined against the stone) is the architect, Frederick W. Waller, and behind him the builder, William Jones.

DICKENS FELLOWSHIP, whose members, dressed as characters from the novels of Charles Dickens, re-enacted scenes or read passages from the books at their meetings. The President of the Gloucester Branch, standing second from the right, was E. Kendall Pearson, for many years the News Editor of the *Citizen*. Third from the right is the President of the Tewkesbury Branch.

# Some Schools and Sports

CRYPT GRAMMAR SCHOOL FOOTBALL CLUB, 1898–9.

CRYPT GRAMMAR SCHOOL, c. 1907.

SIXTH FORM, CRYPT GRAMMAR SCHOOL, 1935.

GREYFRIARS, 1923. This must have been a very familiar sight to Crypt schoolboys as they left school by the side gate into Greyfriars, the former Franciscan Monastery founded 1239, suppressed in 1538. Part of the church was converted into a dwelling-house and wine and spirit vaults.

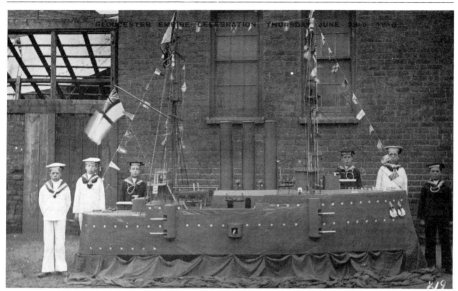

DEACON STREET COUNCIL SCHOOL, 1910. As part of the Empire Celebration, 23rd June, the school made a tableau depicting 'The Navy'.

LONDON ROAD NATIONAL SCHOOL, Standard IV, 1915.

KING'S SCHOOL. The choir was on the roof of the Cathedral as part of the celebrations for King George's coronation, June 1911. Dean Ellacott is in the centre front.

ARCHDEACON STREET SCHOOL RUGBY TEAM, 1925. Standing at back: A. Hawkins (Headmaster), Jones, Rea, Keveren, Pugh, E. Boughton, Mr Harris; second row: Cook, Maysey, Dalby, Thomas; seated: Worrall, Gardner, H. Boughton (Capt.), Coulson, Pitman; in front: Kelly Voyce, Wright. Baker Cup winners in three consecutive seasons, without even a draw to mar their record – 62 games played and won; points for, 2,150; points against, 26. The captain was captain of his school, his city, his county and his country.

GLOUCESTER AMATEURS played at Birmingham Y.M.C.A., 26th December 1908.
Standing: Linesman Hibbins, N. Snow, —, A.A. Derrett, E. Gunn, Linesman W.B. Dix.
Seated: J. Dix, D. Jephson, H.V. Jones, L.F. Dudbridge, H. Bond, J. Poole.

GLOUCESTER CITY SWIMMING AND WATER POLO CLUB, 1911. Back row: E.B. Davies, J.H. Webb, R.M. Parker, C.G.W. Furley (Hon. Sec.), F. Tilton (Baths Supt.). Front row: W.J. Lewis, G. Davis (Sub-Capt.), H. Vickeridge (Capt.), S.A. Pickford, E.W. Jordan (Hon. Treas.), S.E. Darby. Seated: J.B. Shadgett, T.D. Small.

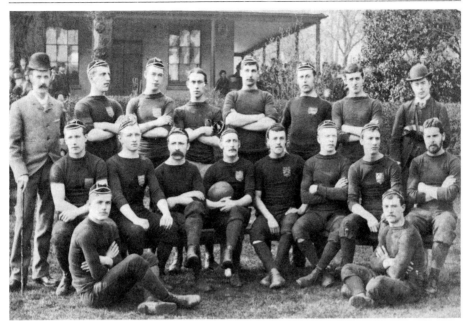

GLOUCESTER FOOTBALL TEAM, 1884–5.

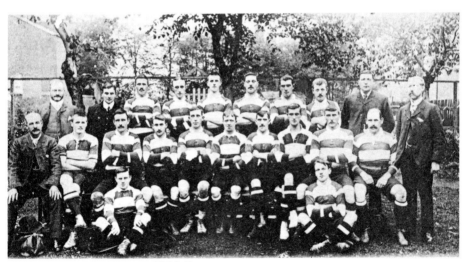

GLOUCESTER FOOTBALL CLUB, 1904–5.

GLOUCESTER OLD BOYS RUGBY FOOTBALL TEAM, season 1913–14. Back row: H. Curtis, N.A. Freeman, J. Gray, A.W. Rowles, D.S. Robertson, A. King. Middle row: P. Simmonds, P.W.S. Aas, S.G. Bennett, W.S. Robertson, L. Smith, R. Gilson, L.H. Peckover, L.S. Price. Front row: J.W. Vance, W. Egerton, M.E.L. Lewis, C.T. Coulson (Capt.), K.A. Robertson, A. Adams, J.M. Baldwin. Seated: T.H.R. Lewis, R.T. Cullis.

MIDLAND RAILWAY FOOTBALL TEAM, GLOUCESTER, 1923–24. The photograph was taken at the Loco-shed at Barnwood which were closed down in 1964. Back row: Albert Robinson, Harold Limbrick, Frank Ford, Bert Houghton, Charlie Hedges, John McCrea, Fred Sutton, Bill Philby. Middle row: Harry Baldwin, —, Ivan Higgs, Charles Lee, Bill Lentovey, L. Butt, Charles Foote, Bob Wilson. Front row: Sidney John Hacker, Sid Bloodworth, Sam Hamer (Capt. Glos. City), Bruce Coates, Harry Sutlow, Frank Wheeler, Frank Bailey, W. Peart, Harry Wicks.

KINGSHOLM TENNIS CLUB. What a picture of elegance the ladies are in their long dresses and wide-brimmed hats. All three courts are in use – perhaps it was tournament.

And afterwards, well-earned refreshments.

GLOUCESTER ROWING CLUB. The boat house on the canal bank, Bristol Road.

# Transport

CO-OP TRANSPORT. Coal deliveries by the Co-op must have been a familiar sight in Gloucester. This photograph shows the Coal Depot in India Road, on an 8½ acre site purchased by the Society in 1883. The coal was brought in on the Midland Railway line from Staffordshire and Leicestershire.

Stables and van shed, India Road, opened 1908.

The Co-op's first steam motor wagon, purchased in 1909.

ELECTRIC TRAMS. The trial trip of the Bristol Road electric tram, 3rd April 1904. The tramcars were double-deckers 25ft long and 6ft 6in wide, the roof deck being 9ft 8in high above the rail. Each car could carry 18 passengers inside and 23 outside. Access to the upper deck was by an open spiral stair.

The depot in Bristol Road could accommodate 50 cars.

There was no upholstery in the interior of the car, plain wooden seats being used. The inside lighting was provided by 6 incandescent lamps – 2 on the roof, 2 on the platforms and 2 on the dashers.

THE CROSS, NORTHGATE–EASTGATE CORNER. Many people watched the men laying the track for the electric trams.

Repairs to the overhead equipment required a strong tower wagon.

DAISY PARDINGTON was one of the first eight tram girls recruited to replace men who had gone to serve in the war in 1914. She is seen here in 1917 with driver S. Gibbins at the Kingsholm terminus.

CITY GARAGE, WORCESTER STREET, c. 1911. J.E. Smith was the first motor repairer in Gloucester. Starting in 1897 he had these premises and 'Cross Garage' in Southgate Street, the interior of which is shown opposite.

FLYING. B.C. Hucks, one of the earliest aviators, gave an exhibition in his Blackburn monoplane in which he reached a height of 1,000 feet. He is seen here at the official welcome on the Port Ham by Mayor James Bruton and the Corporation, 16th October 1911.

GLOUCESTER CARRIAGE AND WHEEL WORKS, established 1846. The showroom on the corner of London Road and George Street – taken over by the Post Office sorting office in 1907.

Inside the photograph, on the left sign:

WAGON MADE BY THE
GLOUCESTER RAILWAY CARRIAGE & WAGON C⁰ L⁰
SHIPPED TO SOUTH AFRICA PER S/S MAJESTIC
DEC. 9 1899 AND USED BY EARL ROBERTS
DURING THE CAMPAIGN IN SOUTH AFRICA
KINDLY LENT BY HIS LORDSHIP

On the right sign:

GLOUCESTER
RAILWAY CARRIAGE
& WAGON C⁰ L^TD
NOVEMBER 1901
PHOTO 2414

A wagon made by the Gloucester Railway Carriage & Wagon Co. Ltd, shipped to South Africa on S.S. *Majestic*, 9th December 1899, and used by Earl Roberts during the campaign there.

E. GOODWIN, FUNERAL DIRECTOR, 222, Barton Street.

*GREAT WESTERN* IN THE DOCKS, 19th August 1899. Howard Blackburn had sailed this 30 foot sloop single-handed from Gloucester, Massachusetts on 18th June. A remarkable feat, especially for this man who had lost all his fingers, half of each thumb and most of his toes.

STEAMER TRIP leaving Westgate Bridge for Lower Lode, Tewkesbury, 1908. Under Captain Sam Priday's management the *Windsor Castle* and *Berkeley Castle* ran daily at 9 a.m. and 3 p.m. for a return fare of 1s. 6d.

Midland Railway Station, Gloucester.

MIDLAND RAILWAY STATION. Now occupied by ASDA Superstores.

THE MAIN BASIN OF THE DOCKS crowded with sailing vessels, probably in the 1880s.

STRETTON CYCLE AND MOTOR ENGINEER. Established 1895 at the top of Worcester Street with offices on one side and the showroom on the other.

TAYLORS OF GLOUCESTER. Founded in 1925, Taylors moved their premises in Worcester Street from the building on the extreme left to this new garage where they stayed until 1981, until removing to Bristol Road.

THE INAUGURATION OF THE HORSE TRAMS, 1880. The opening procession, complete with flags and spectators, in Southgate Street. The trams ran along Northgate, Southgate and Eastgate Streets and continued in use until 1904 when the electric tram was introduced.

TRAFFIC IN WESTGATE STREET APPROACHING THE CROSS, c. 1930.

# ACKNOWLEDGEMENTS

I welcome this opportunity to express my thanks to the many people who have helped me in the compilation of this volume, especially the County Librarian, Mr Bernard Stradling, for allowing me to use the Gloucestershire Collection. Librarians have always sought to collect material relating to their immediate locality, but to decide in 1900, when Gloucester Library was opened, to collect such a wide range of material for the entire County of Gloucestershire showed fantastic foresight, and it is fitting here to acknowledge both the foresight and enthusiasm of city and county councillors, librarians, local historians and members of the public in founding and maintaining this now prestigious Collection. A measure of the quality of the Collection is that this volume is the third book of Gloucester photographs to be drawn exclusively from that Collection. As Local History Librarian I fully appreciate the skill and dedication of former librarians, especially Roland Austin, Douglas Aldridge and Victor Woodman, who have produced very detailed indexes to the Collection, which make the task of looking for minute pieces of information so very much easier.

The mainstay of the original photographic Collection were the photographs of Arthur and Sidney Pitcher taken as part of a record survey of the changing face of Gloucester. This work is continued today by the Royal Commission on Historical Monuments (England) who have very kindly allowed me to use copies of photographs in the Gloucestershire Collection for which they hold the copyright. For the section on disasters the newspapers are almost the only source, and I am indebted to the *Gloucester Journal* and the *Cheltenham Chronicle and Gloucestershire Graphic* for the use of their photographs.

Five people in particular, who share my love of old photographs, have given very generously their time and knowledge – my colleague Rosealeen Lane, Mr Anthony Done who has produced his own index of Gloucester photographs and is now indexing the Gloucester items from the *Gloucester Journal*, Mr Arthur Dodd of the Civic Trust, my husband Ron who has reproduced many lantern slides for inclusion in this book, and Miss Elizabeth Bullock who typed the captions.

Finally may I thank those people who have provided information for a specific photograph – Mr Brian Frith, Mr Philip Moss, Mr Brian Powell, Miss D.A.K. Pearson, Mr R.V. Parsons, Mr J. Ridler, Mrs O.W. Vallender, Mr and Mrs Price and Mr Oliver Watkins.

JILL VOYCE